COMMON

Theophilus Kwek is a writer, editor and translator based in Singapore. His work has been published in *The Guardian, Times Literary Supplement, The Straits Times*, and elsewhere; and performed at the Royal Opera House. Two of his previous collections of poetry were shortlisted for the Singapore Literature Prize, while his pamphlet, *The First Five Storms*, won the inaugural New Poets' Prize. In 2023, he was the youngest writer and first Singaporean to be awarded the Cikada Prize by the Swedish Institute, for poetry that 'defends the inviolability of life'. He is a member of the Folio Academy, and part of the Forbes 30 Under 30 Class of 2024.

COMMON
WEALTH

Theophilus Kwek

CARCANET POETRY

First published in Great Britain in 2025 by
Carcanet
Main Library, The University of Manchester
Oxford Road, Manchester, M13 9PP
www.carcanet.co.uk

A CIP catalogue record for this book is
available from the British Library.

ISBN 978 1 80017 483 2

Book design by Andrew Latimer, Carcanet
Typesetting by LiteBook Prepress Services
Printed in Great Britain by SRP Ltd, Exeter, Devon

MIX
Paper | Supporting
responsible forestry
FSC® C014540

The publisher acknowledges financial
assistance from Arts Council England.

Supported using public funding by
ARTS COUNCIL
ENGLAND

For Cherie –
everything in common.

CONTENTS

Commonwealth: A Geography   10

PART ONE

PART TWO

PART THREE

'A pile of stones: an assertion
that this piece of country matters
for large and simple reasons.'

Adrienne Rich

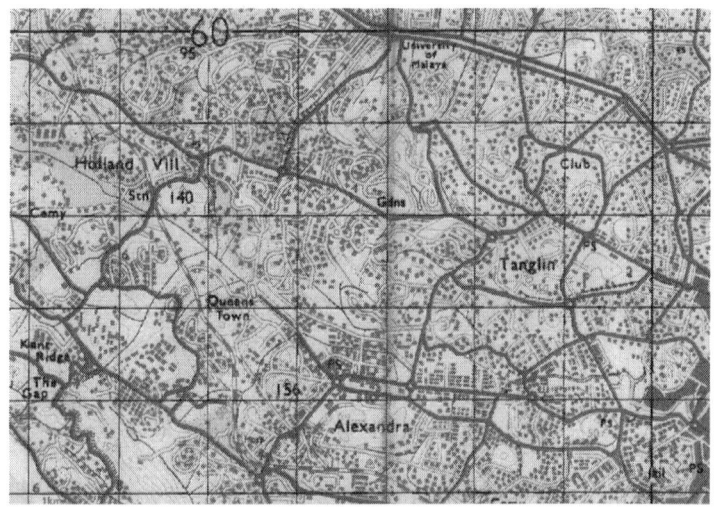

The district of Commonwealth, Singapore, and its neighbourhoods; 1963.

Accession No. TM000974, Courtesy of the National Archives of Singapore.

PART ONE

CLOSING TIME

'Tanglin Halt's tenants [...] will need to move out of their
hawker stalls and shops in seven years.'
— TODAY, 4 July 2014

Enough time, it seems, for a reckoning,
to scrape the grounds from the bottoms of our cups
and sweep stacked cups from their tables
as at the end of a night's reminiscing

to turn the benches over to the birds
already sentry among the half-filled seats
for what's left from the helpings uneaten,
chess-games unfinished, tall tales unheard,

to draw shutters over the LED signs
beaming comfort from their hack-wired frames,
throw out flattened sticks of sugar-cane
strung with the last of our raffia twine,

strip out the lights that for now, still smoulder
with a ghostly joy though the current's still,
charged as on our first day with the thrill
of something built, and something brighter.

CLEARANCES

We have had our clearances too:

I.

Our high landings and their enclosures,
        our stiff paper slapped
onto the doors. Fine chairs in stairwells

too heavy to lift, the quality of their wood
        unimpeachable.
They say teak grows thickest in the tropics,

soaks silica from the sand, blunts the tools
        that shape it. All that grit
in the grain. In some countries the trees

are sown as firebreak, as in some versions
        of this tale, where on
the fateful night the Sultan's dancing-hall

burned, his servants' quarters – fine timber –
        survived. In their prime
the Tyersall grounds were second to none,

horses and motor-cars tearing up the tracks.
        Imagine, to have had
the colony's first telephone installed, and still

lose your calls in a flood of hoofbeats. First
          to come, as things began
to go south, were the Argyll and Sutherland

Highlanders; then the Marines, their mettle
          by then already lost
with Churchill's best ships in the South China Sea.

Barracked on empire's great bowling-green,
          the day they marched
to Changi not one of the Sultan's children

cheered. A bitter trade, this: one conquest
          for another, change
of title and the deed forever done. But here

          too, and before all that –

II.

A man named Napier built a house. *Tang Leng,*
      Tanglin. Etymology uncertain,
            first mentioned in '47, and in
                  the paper Napier made. *Yesterday*

it said, *a female tiger was brought to town*
      killed in Tangling district. Here again,
            '57: the residence of one
                  William Napier, Esquire, in Tang Leng

District – *terraced walks and shrubberies* –
      For Sale. *Planted with an avenue of trees.*
            By this time the East had quite lost its ease,
                  the man himself no more at his rajah's

right hand. But as one Napier waned another
      came by the death of an Earl to rule
            all India. A promotion from Madras
                  for sure, some would say *sinecure.* From there

to a lordship, then a Scottish estate
      and later still, a task for steady hands:
            a Royal Commission. *On the Condition*
                  of Crofters in the Highlands and Islands.

No matter the climate. In that distant
      parallel, a people so familiar –
            less precious in their English landlords' eyes
                  than the land their landlords spied. Small wonder

rebellion still smoulders in the gorse.
    Year after year, and barely a stone's throw
        from *the Hill on which the house is built,*
          an extensive and pleasing prospect

the Ceylon leaves sit cooling in their cups
    doused with milk tinned for the boys abroad,
        waiting for a crack of knuckles against wood
          and the voice of a man who knew your order.

III.

What I don't understand is the order of things.

The giving and taking of land, the sleight of hand
by which a railway is turned into a garden
and then the gardeners too, trimmed and transplanted
to a nearby plot. (Well-watered: *Stirling, Strathmore...*
the estate is rife with rivers.) All along, was *this*
the plot? I search the beds for answers. In '52,
with a faith to match their Queen's, they named
the blocks here before they stood. *Alexandra,*
Margaret. Just how much was foreseen? It's said
Elizabeth was happiest in the highlands: now
consider, how Albert bought Balmoral without
so much as a viewing, house and servants intact
in order to give Victoria her bonny view.
What a gift! *Mei Ling, Mei Chin.* (But was it also
from this that she came to develop her appetite
for acquisitions?) Already, posters proclaim
new life in Dawson, though some there would insist
on keeping others away from its bonniest heights.
This side of Commonwealth, like hills shorn of houses –
the better to graze the whitest wool – the roads
seem blessed with quieter names. *Barbary, Merino,*
Angora. Only minutes from where a longer
silence falls, it's easy to mistake the builders' noise
for that of things being built, a din not at all
unlike life itself. Listen: *this* is gain, and *this*,
loss. One the water's course, and one the source.

IV.

But wait, look. The paper will not stay.

How it flaps, flags as torn paint flakes away,
beats its own limp verse against the wood.

Writing on the wall already faint,
it gives notice to whoever will listen –

I have this day taken possession!

As published in the Government Gazette!

– like a madman yelling by the market
so loud, you could've heard it by the tracks.

Birds flock at the sound. What is this,
that has made a zoo of their neighbourhood?

Even the trees shake their leaves, displeased.
Of the three corners that have come unstuck

one makes its case most insistently,
says –

As needed for a public purpose!

– so sure it is of its business here.
(The windows, which no longer open, sneer.

They too have seen purposes in their time,
as have the railings and bamboo-poles

freed now from the weight of wet linen.)
Soon, the wind will do as the wind does.

A sort of quiet will rest again
against the door, its faults and ridges

a record of all who have come, gone.
Notice: there will be room here

for more than quiet. More than light
sweeps its hand across the floor.

THE SEER

There he knelt,
laying out his implements
on a sheet – a knife,
paper, some lemons –

as the circle
tightened around him,
sleeve-to-sleeve
under the thin awning.

The first, who
asked about his daughter
went away believing,
holding his answer

like a charm
and soon the change
began to appear, a miracle
in the borrowed bowl.

Of all the wonders
done that morning, in the lie
of the makeshift shade,
it seemed only

the most ordinary
thing for the planets,
not far above, to draw close,
leaving their orbits,

stand still, and for
a vanishing hour crane
their necks over an old
faithful star.

JALAN BESAR

See how it swells from the brown surface:
the land curving above the world's own curve

something to stand on, a turbulent plot
leading nowhere but this heart of swampy ground.

An inheritance. For less than a hundred
and twenty rupees the marsh changed hands,

was burnt to brick, was drenched and planted over,
named *Lavender* to mask its loamy stench

then named again, a scorch of distant fires,
every inch of road a confrontation.

Allenby, Jellicoe, Kitchener, Foch –
streets stamped sturdily into

a New World founded from the ash,
the best opera in Malaya opening

to the tap of the taxi-girls' feet. Years
later they saw their young gather here

to mourn and dance, shin-deep in rain rising
from beneath grass to claim its lawful turf,

lift the lowered shutters and make their way.
Who walks it now? One day, perhaps, we'll find

we were reading it wrong. Not as a name
or station, but in a voice river-clear

and full with history's silt: no small step,
to stride wide upon the earth, and leave a mark.

THE GARDENER

Transplanted here, I had just days to learn
their ways, which ones grew gangly against
a wall, which took to sunshine, which sprang
from roots so strong they turned the paving-stones,

and names, all grafted from tongue to tongue,
cengkih, angsana, tembusu, gelam.
I watched and watered. Was slow to prune
what seemed peculiar or out of place, limbs

ungainly among the others, stooped
to tease each fractious shadow from the soil.
After dark I'd search in vain (or hope)
for a day's headway, but find them just as tall

as when I began. No-one told me then
what years have taught me about the night –
how gently it comes, to stay the hand.
They do their best growing when out of sight.

STUDIO PHOTOGRAPH OF A CHINESE MAN IN FANCY COSTUME

Lee Brothers Studio Collection, c. 1920

Nine in the morning and November clouds
blooming softly behind the shophouses.

*

Mr Lee curses his luck, curses the clouds,
runs his hand across a tattered row of screens.

Lingers.

     A boy leaps up to haul the cord
that slides another room into place, rich red
curtains pulled back, a chaste rosebush
masking the false window.   Everyone knows
his brother has opened another studio
on Stamford Road – trust the old fox
to book the Governor's picture at lunchtime,
nobody could miss that big car leaving.
Outside: a siren, the clatter of boots
               Hold still! says Mr Lee
as the new fire station pours out its men
onto the street. Mr Lee looks at me like he knows
what I'm thinking.   *Dr Sun came and sat
in my chair, didn't he? The same one you're in.*
This I can't deny. Another boy enters the room,
laughs, splits my hair like an orange. I feel
my elbow stiffen against the arm of my seat,
Mr Lee's white frock tight around the neck.
              Look here, now –

*

"Back then, years passed when you wouldn't pose for a picture. If someone tried to take your picture, even if it was meant to be silly or spontaneous, you still fussed and awkwardly posed, because there was a finality to it… Later, when photography became ubiquitous, pictures were evidence that you existed at all."

– Hua Hsu, Stay True

*

The boy places a lute in my lap, brings my fingers
to the frets. I look ridiculous, I'm sure of it.

What size?   Mr Lee again.
What size?   Barking this time.

                 Eight ten,
I manage to say. He sucks in his lip
noisily above the camera's click and whirr
then straightens, satisfied, and is gone.
The rest, it appears, is the boy's work – who,
as I loosen the britches around my thighs,
feel beneath the tips of my collar to match
each hook and eye, pulls the glass plates
without looking from the machine's little door
and carries them downstairs to take the light.

         *

"She says in the end the picture is everything. Nobody looks at the [thing] themselves."

– Shubigi Rao, Talking Leaves

         *

Later, I hardly recognise myself. It isn't just
that nobody has a room like this *(satin drapes –
in Singapore!)*, more how everything seems
to recede, soft beams glancing off the roofs
on Hill Street to paint the foreground. Whose
is this body the sitter's chair holds like an inch
of dust?
              I think of the other room
where, away from the glare of those
high windows, a pair of gentle hands lowers
the negatives into clear solvent, sets free
a likeness held in place by the sun.
                   Of Mr Lee
and his brother, both jealous of the city's eye,
of the image, fainter now, who is both me and
not-me, and the other ways light takes to arrive.

KONG

i.m. Emile Czaja aka 'King Kong'

They called him King. Other names came later –
Samson, Hercules – but this one stuck, a name
he could twirl overhead as the crowd cheered,
one with its own weight-class. No longer 'Emile',
they trembled at the *thud* as he took the stage,
made short work of the others (Tiger Ahmad,
Gorilla Wong…), the whole Great World rising
to their feet. Even Wildcat Hassan, who in '47
had gone up against the star of the British base
was no match: everyone knew the ring belonged
to the boy from Budapest with brazen hands.
Backstage, another world was being formed
in the sharp shadows of those stadium lamps,
each lock and throw an echo of the long night's
hold, slipping surely into morning. By the time
he wound up at *si-pai-por*, pulled from a car's
steel grip, his own gnarled fingers loosening,
the realm he knew had ceded title to another.
A clean flip, it happened right before his eyes.
Years later they said they hadn't seen it coming.

QUARANTINE

'Amid beautiful Tembusu trees stood some government hol-
iday bungalows... [one] was ringed with chain link topped
with barbed wire. This housed the political detainees.'
– Lee Kuan Yew, 1952

Half an hour's sail from the shore, no more,
a square meal put away, a span of sleep
without dreaming. An island is a door

through which a sea is strung, famished lip
of land caught between the country's teeth,
a spool for the waves. This is how they keep

what must be kept at bay: on a reef
made fast with a brace of trees, like a fence
fine enough that it stays unseen, or a sieve,

not made to hold but to wear us thin. Once
our fathers came, fleeing death to death,
marooned so the barrenness would cleanse

their bodies' dread, while not a hand's breadth
away their betters ate and slept – exempt
by wealth or whiteness, more often both.

Now in their place, we who have neither bide
our time, nurse our hereditary rage,
and watch for a turning in the southern tide

that scours this rock daily around the edge
but spares what springs unruly from the sand;
our banyan, mangrove, mastwood, sedge.

*'Some have posited that the region referred to in ancient
texts as Suvarnabhumi most likely applied to the historical
kingdom of Funan…' – Asian Geographic*

In late February, their scribes will say,
clouds hang low enough overhead
that those tending to the gardens lengthwise
along the tower's eastern edge swear
they keep the branches from bruising the sky.

*

Next door, wise men of the kingdom weigh
a country's worth in trays of gold
that never empty. This wonder brings
the princes and their poets, who are prophets
too of a most fantastical kind.

*

A mountain glowers at the tower's heart
like a shard, which day after day
cuts the hands of those who dare to scale it.
High above, the kingdom's children play
on grassy slopes that never winter.

*

Around the gates on Sunday mornings
sit the sons of an ancient prince,
with shoulders blistered from the tower's bricks.
Worry crowns them about the brows.
The only throne they're offered is the earth.

*

Cross-legged, they contemplate this odd
reflecting tower, its mudstained sides,
wash its newest names through older tongues:
Phnom. Phù Nam. Fúnán. Funan.
These too come and go, a slower tide.

SENTENCE

There's a scientific explanation
for most things
             like how life, as they say,
flickers into view moments from the end
or how the soul slips the body briefly –
a sneeze, then dark – but
                          for what he saw
that early bright afternoon as it fell
with a clang about him, sky cold as steel
flinching from the sea as if in shock
and the waves
             with a dash of alchemy
turning to iron as he was, then wasn't
a shadow stretched over their salt surface
has still not been found
                          any known cause
nor sequence from which we might begin
to derive some hypothesis, some guess
towards a truth…
             no, merely the report
of his mouth which was seen, as he toppled
from the bow into a stretch of channel
uneasily held
             between two territories,
to be holding in its yell the start
of some unspoken sentence, an opening
that could be imagined
                          by some of those
who saw the shape of him falling, and knew
something of the deep that would come,
to be the same syllable
                          that they too
heard, too often, and hated, and understood.

PARABLE OF FEET AND WINGS

They're at it again, the pair of them,
scuttle and cackle and scuttle and hiss,
spooky because it's coming through
the rolled-up poster I've stashed behind
my desk. All month long, nights flush
with hot rain, then first thing you see
the room's four corners slick with wings,
bones from a feast. From somewhere
down the labyrinth that's under my bed –
a guilty laugh. Or not: nature's appetite,
says Dad, as he sweeps the glistening
film off the floor. Each perfect teardrop
snapped at the stem, a parachute made
to land a body somewhere safe or catch
a drift of tropical air above a reading-
lamp. Here, you'd best get used to it.
The cloud of ants, the geckoes' joy,
small carnage. That's all there is to it.

*

I think of a time when, clothed unwillingly
in green, I stood sentry for a night in
a whitewashed post watching the shut
gates of the camp. Just keeping awake,
barely, the sharp knob of a rifle's scope
slung against my ribs. Across the hard
grey square of the floor with their heads
bitten clean were the carcasses of ants –
often, with feet and wings intact. The

culprits? They made a whole show of it:
now slouching in wait beneath the light's
bare electric coil, now tussling in full
view over a spent creature's parts. Not
for any lack but seemingly, the fun of it.
When the sky softened into morning
the others found me still transfixed,
by the sight of the night's last travellers
falling, exhausted, then hauled away.

*

Harmless, really. And even sometimes a
picture of good, the way they build whole
civilisations out of the soil. Industrious.
Not without grounds, our own distrust
builds – against their flightier cousins who
shimmer about the lights. In the dimming
years of Empire, some would later say,
the chandeliers at the Raffles ballroom
had never burned so bright. Oh, look how
they burned. In the days that followed
we learned nothing lasts in these parts
except what takes to the earth unseen,
gnaws through mud till the foundations
hold. (Not in this heat anyway, which
has felled kings and their men.) I digress.
It is the heat that draws both geckoes and
their prey, long-limbed and free, the ones
still dancing when the lights go out.

*

Imagine my surprise when I found out
that these winged apparitions were not
a different breed. When the storms come,
a colony has two choices. Lose the walls
and chambers of their mud-slicked nest
to wet decay, or send their best sojourners
out – doves from an ark – that elsewhere
some hardy offshoot of their own might
burrow, thrive. A mystery, if only to our
earthbound eyes, that love by any other
name is flight. (So much more vicious
now in this light appears the geckoes'
appetites! Though this too, may be a trick
of the eyes.) Stoop close and see. How
fraught and, unburdened by metaphor,
how free: each whip of a tail, each graceful
taking to the air; which ones each season
leave earth behind, and yet are there.

COMMONWEALTH

In one of the photographs there's a girl
who can't be older than eleven or twelve

dressed for the occasion in a white frock
and socks to match, hoicked high, black

shoes in a 'V' on the road's black tar
which has just opened from Queensway

to Alexandra. Or, *is being opened* – this
being a time when roads are still opened

with cameras and speeches, a Minister
in tow, though all eyes are on that seam

of earth scabbed over – a clean crust, like
new ice on a river. She's ducked beneath

the tape that marks where the road begins,
tape that for now holds the onlookers back

except coming barely to her shoulders it
lets her right through, past all the elbows

to where the action is. Not that you can tell
from the photograph, of course (in some

ways I think you had to be there), a scene
of more than soil cleared away, more

than tar poured out on the carriageway.
There she is, now and forever too, fixed

at this opening in time before what comes
after: light industry, a city on its heels,

so quick even the grownups are caught
by surprise. The same grownups tiptoeing

now for all that's still unseen, caught here
in a blink of a lens. Yes, an industry of light.

PART TWO

RELOCATIONS

a record

I.

THE BEGINNING

What would you save if your house was on fire?
It is the first week of school and we are to answer

this question, introduce ourselves over the din
of the pub. *One thing you'd grab from a burning*

room. We take it in turns: the family cat, books,
a hard drive full of holidays. Someone sets a glass

down – too quickly – so the shadows jump, and I
see Big Aunt hoist my mother below the arms,

turn, and with uncommon grace make for the highest
ground. *How about you?* I see their faces, bright

with expectation, know that none of this will bear
re-telling, not here or now. They are waiting for

a story, and not one that goes: *we have had a fire*
in the family. That evening's still bright, years later,

and their faces still aglow, as staring out the open
window I find myself unsure of how to begin.

II.

DELIVERY

We were never what you might call, poor.
My father ran the provisions shop

and a fleet of lorries, and when the flames
came they packed the women and children

on them and drove and drove. I remember
it was a public holiday, so all

the men were home, doing repairs, odd jobs…
some even hoping for one more call

to make the month's cheque. No-one
could have guessed, but the call that came

through that afternoon was to be their most
fragile delivery. Some lost everything,

others had everything taken. But no, not
even then. You would not have called us poor.

III.

YOUR PAINS ARE THE PAINS OF OUR GOVERNMENT

And your joy, your happiness are the joy
and happiness of our government. This

is the truth. So let us all face the truth
together. Whoever started this fire

is a heartless person, it was a heartless
person who started this fire. Our government

definitely did not start this fire. Who
started this fire would not have come

to this place, would not dare to come and face
the truth – but look, we are here. The night

we knew of the fire, our Prime Minister
was here. He announced that the fire was

very serious, and after he said this,
immediately we started work. The next day

again he was here, and he told everyone
to support our brothers and sisters, in

this Bukit Ho Swee and Tiong Bahru
calamity. I say to you again. Your pains

are the pains of our government. Your joy
and your happiness are our joys.

IV.

ZINC

No one knows how it happens. No one knows how it
happens. No one knows how it happens. It happens
like this: a father builds a pond in the red earth. Fills it

with fish – half a year's savings – which will sell for
more in a few months. Rain washes poison off their zinc
roof, killing the fish, but he tries again: builds a rack,

runs a length of fresh tarpaulin over the side. Within
days the fire, envious, comes. His oldest daughter runs
up a slope, a girl on her back, her brothers close behind

and carrying whatever they can. There is no saving
the house, or its treacherous roof, even the fish, that will
be singed into the earth. For years afterwards he drives

the graveyard shift, watches the sky for rain, saves
the pomfret at dinner once a month for his littlest one.
Or so my mother, who still loves the fish, remembers.

V.

PASAR

On the clearest nights from the tallest floors
you can still see the dragon's tail of it
laid out against the night's extravagance

swaddling the old church river of light
a thousand small fires dancing on the gas
see the first red roof of the neighbourhood

raised above the swamp where pastor Nga
used to tell the story of his lost left shoe
swallowed by the earth before all this land

was piled firm enough for them to build on
houses to hold every one of us
corridors stacked right into the sky

how we loved those long and endless railings
taking our first steps high up in the air
the new grey stone still sticky underfoot

till the earth returned us to the ground
brought us back out on the hottest nights
aunty Hasmah with her fresh bowls of ice

her kerosene lamp a lighthouse above
our heads the crowd pressed behind and all
around us the river radiant everywhere

MID AUTUMN

Last time after six you see all the children
go down to the tracks hold their lantern
not like the kind you see today got light
got battery last time is use cellophane
red blue orange wrap around the bamboo
make rabbit make aeroplane make 包青天
like from the TV show yah very colourful

nearby all the shops the market can see
they will hang the lantern along outside
so we will come every child holding one
lighter one packet of candles wah the most
exciting time so we will all come and see
and choose our lantern everyone choose
this year which character they want to be

young that time don't have those luxury
you know today that kind of game so these
are the things we do light candle go down
to the railway because dark better to see
so many things I will forget but this one
like brand new like that our childhood fun
now you don't know now very sad already

VII.

give notice under the powers
conferred upon me by the act
section 16 cap 152
revised edition 1985

I have

this day taken possession of
this strata lot no 868-G-7
otherwise known block 56
commonwealth drive 07-58

that is referred to

as needed for a public purpose
as published in the government gazette
no 26 notification 1654 viz
selective en bloc redevelopment scheme

a notice

of possession signed the collector
of land revenue care
of HDB Hub Lorong 6 Toa Payoh 310480 Republic
of Singapore

VIII.

TANGLIN, HALT

Sunday afternoon, and the market empty.
'Happy 57th National Day'
proclaims a banner hung up for no one
as sheets of paper bang the padlocked doors.

Elsewhere, Red Lions are falling from the sky.
Here a flag riots in the August heat,
trapped mid-flutter by a bamboo rack.
Ferns run amok along the walls' crevasses,

overthrow the tiles from their brick-red roofs.
Now and then, a wasp dares to clamour against
the sweetness of my cup. Something has possessed
the estate, filled it with the sort of quiet

that would wake a child. Disbelieving,
pigeons mob the square, raise grievances
in voices long and loud. Stripped of its leather,
a cobbler's old seat rallies the crowd.

NO TAIL RIVER

Alexandra Canal ('Boh Beh Kang')

A shuffling of tiles, or the shaking out
of an old flat. The sound comes to my ears

in waves, the way sound travels in age,
ungainly and unsure. A lift dings twice

or a bicycle, so I brace myself
against the green railings. They go by so

quickly these days, the young, hot on their wheels.
Remember how when we first moved in

the blocks jutted out in their eagerness,
squeezing the path behind the wet edge

of the school? Somewhere, men are already
laying down new beams, like tongues of a bell.

The school I think is now a show flat which,
as my son who went there says, is a much

better use of the space. He isn't
even joking, though these days it can

be so hard to tell. Just yesterday I took
the neighbour's cane for someone outside,

was quite sure when he came *knock-knock*ing down
the corridor. The kids want me to move,

but I won't hear of it. I've always said:
this place has a magic to it. How softly

the river goes – how still, like a well!
How quickly a koel's cry becomes a child's.

THE SWIMMERS

Bukit Merah Swimming Complex

I.

Soft strong scoop of the palms, a forehead
breaking water, followed by the body
of a child. More than the hop and dive,
this is the moment she trains herself

to look out for: something from nothing,
a shadow under the water's skin
turning wet and real, emerging. Hourly
the dull shriek of the whistle, unheeded,

a dance of feet against the surface
and with each stroke the water-tousled crowns
drowned then surfacing, alive, alive,
alive. Behind her the lockers beam

their proprietary gleam, flecked with what
the swimmers' hands deliver from the deep.
Marauding joy like the push of water,
high, scouring sunlight, a tang of bleach.

II.

Her youngest already seventeen,
these days she finds the house too quiet –
at least, that's what she tells them when they ask.
The pool knows nothing of quiet, laps

incessantly with a tide of children
released from towels flung carelessly by.
Repeatedly she wipes the reddish tiles
though at the end of the hour like clockwork

they pour back inside, lithe as fish, and
her locker-room becomes a shallow sea.
These are her catch. For them she will lay out
the mats over and over, make ritual

of repetition. She knows their seasons
and tempers, how they itch for the water,
shiver when hauled onto land. In the shade
of the hill she squeezes her towels dry.

III.

Never the superstitious sort, she pays
little heed to those who say there must
be something amiss. *Mm zai si! Brave
of them to knock down the temple – for this!*

Braver, she thinks, the ones who come to test
the depths, their wagers of thirty cents left
clinking on her counter. No matter their
peals of laughter, joy rising afterwards,

it is the quick negating plunge that stays
most difficult, the leap to silence
that all children at first are scared of.
And then to do it ten, a hundred times,

to weave between the waking and the dead
a line sinuous as earth, the water
making way... She shuts her eyes, listens
for their slippered feet like cards being shuffled.

IV.

Watching, the hours turn to days, days months.
She becomes accustomed to the water's
pull, the way it holds her gaze, like a lure.
On wet afternoons the building empties

and there is only the spell of water
crowning on water, the top of the pool
a cloud-scattered field put out to flower.
At the unguarded end of the year

it is the same, the whole complex silent,
except now a calmness takes the surface
that is of a kind with daybreak
announcing itself along the corridor.

Still in the dip and swell she sees them,
their long arms partitioning the air
and every last niche on the wall behind
packed again with all their dry belongings.

YELLOWTOP

Twenty years ago this would've been his job.
Crossing the island on an afternoon
with rain coming down like how it used to,
enough to fill a pond newly-dug
with promise from the sky, slippery as fish,
in his yellowtop to ferry one of the children

to some happy event or the other –
third uncle home for dinner after booking out
or mother with her two styrofoams of coffee,
one for the boy who becomes my father.
Always with his eyes on the road ahead,
those deep puddles parting to let his tyres through

but today I remember he's on his way elsewhere,
a trip called in so suddenly
it took us by surprise. Not that he complained,
settling himself quietly behind the wheel
as he always did, knowing he'd be right on time:
so just this once, it's me waiting for grandma

at the foot of the block where they've sent me off
so many times I have to look again
to convince myself he isn't there.
Waiting with both windows down as I think
he would've done, the better to see every one
of our faces now appearing on the other side.

THIS YEAR

the world does not welcome us as it ought,
with green bunting blazing from the boughs
or feathered things suddenly appearing.

No, no. Such assurances are for those
who have never heard a siren downstairs,
nor fear, ascending with a neighbour's voice.

Roaming the squares of our kitchens and desks,
we are soon lost. Walls mask themselves against
the sky's pale tower, and there is birdsong

in the plaintive swinging of the doors. Still
it comes to us – the world – through a window's
dull gash, with branches drier than kindling

and sketched in light. Bereft as we are
it sidles into view, then sings and sings, fills
enough of the room to give us sight.

PEARL BANK

1976–2019

The pillars, too, regret this.
The columns are full of outcry, staircases
weep, and the glass doors,
whose wheels are still running in their tracks.

In the driveway, left in haste,
are possessions too big for the moving-van:
a bedframe, a mahjong table
with its tiles discarded, a winning hand.

After this morning's rain,
a smell of death has come to roost among
the debris. Look closely,
someone has emptied out the living,

out here, onto the street.
It is a difficult thing, to see a building
gape, and gape even wider
than the gap between its two front teeth.

Maybe it was the architecture
that singled it out. *Socialist,*
so, unfit for our times.
No room now for rooms like these,

level lives, a piece of God's
blue sky for everyone. Capital, land –
the price has changed
though old factors remain. *What, then?*

something new must come.
There will be rain again, and rain over
the earth, till another grain
sleeps, wakes, becomes a pearl.

SENIORS' ACTIVITY CORNER

Late-night TV mimes on-screen, while rain
pools unnoticed in the lumpy grass. I'm
out again, sleepless, when I see them
on a long thin bench holding court, minding

their own business. *Nothing's changed,* says
Melchior, slapping the stone table
so as to get the last word, though Caspar
isn't letting him have it. *Naw, it's always*

the same with you, gloomy git! (And
here Balthazar chimes in,) *world hasn't
quite ended yet, has it?* Round and round
they go, these three – kings of all there is –

as doors shut, the children climb to their beds,
and further yet, a lone star rises, sets.

FLYOVER

I.

When was it I learned that two

roads, one going this, one the other way
could meet here, for a time run parallel

to the sky, and reaching down (as if both
were to lean on one shoulder) rest their palms

against the earth, their single steadying
shadow like a handstand, or a prayer?

I remember how on winter nights
in Manchester my own parents, draping

a blanket between them, would by the light
of a torch kindle a whole room, cover

the walls with dragons. Today, you let
your fingers dangle by your side, knowing

already that they will find their mirror
in mine. Walking among the tall pillars,

we fall into step. Above our heads
like distant thunder traffic goes and goes.

II.

Look! What comes from cracks in the concrete,
a weakness that cars ran and still run over.
Here a branch, a sprig of leaves unfolding,
there a sound like a first beating of wings.

It takes less than we think. A bit of earth
caught in the struts, an afternoon's downpour
then sun, to do as the sun does. Yet
also more: the unseen hand that sweeps each
journeying seed to land, moulds a bridge
into a fist to catch this throw of the wind.
Pedestrians hardly notice,

                but *look*, you say,

and draw my eyes upwards and higher still
beyond the green untangling from the crook
of the bridge, to where cement gives way
to metal, metal gives way to air, and held
aloft there by the same invisible
force, a pair – like us – though falling, rises.

III.

Taking my hand, you walk
into the house of light,
its steeple reaching up
between two lanes without
so much as a rivet
to hold each beam in place.

From this bright aisle a palm
sends up its newest leaves
uxorious for the sun
while the columns themselves
haul heavenward like trees
whose huddled canopies

cannot contain the spray
of bougainvillea
from their highest branches.
If ever it should seem
that our shared carriageway
turns uphill underfoot

remember how we stood
briefly in the quiet
beneath another road –
how soft the earth's carpet,
how blue the sky's stained glass
unseen except from here.

CORRIDOR

Old KTM tracks

The raintrees' dance takes lifetimes, years
longer than our music, passing in quick step,
is sovereign to itself, oblivious
of events and, by its own slow grace,

      invisible. At this edge of the estate
      they rise at arms' length, toes to the line
      to keep every heel and turn,
      so practiced are they in their variations

that even now, in the silence of the rails
their branches still stretch by habit
across the aisle. Forgetting themselves,
each comes within a breath of another's crown

      then stops, carrying in its spread fingers' shade
      an imprint of the next living thing, as
      sky enters unannounced, a bare
      blue river in between. Nothing wanes

this force of life in them. More than
time has covered the tracks, and on either side
saved for a while, a seam of someone else's
land unfolds into green. No wonder

      the quiet still kneels to meet us here,
      a sanctuary so familiar. We walk
      with an unaccustomed ease, not touching,
      our joy is the joy of trees.

ROAD WORKS

Bukit Brown

How weird, you say, as it shakes itself
from the hill's green rug to look at us,
sharing a pew on the 165 turning
onto Lornie and safe, for now, behind glass.

How like a river, is what I think you mean,
forgetting its place on the forest floor,
a miracle, even. The sea scarfed back
as in Moses's time to let our people through,

unblemished. I wonder what tale they'll tell
years from now, when our children's children fly
glass taxis above the road and steel
holding a wound open beneath their feet,

of how we shaved our own country bare,
slipped, were left with the tender slope of it.
Nothing will pave the rough earth over,
but think! How doubtless we were then, how sure –

our words lending their sly heft to the fact
of us driving our feet down into the dirt,
turning up the dead, and with bare hands
building this thing, this irreparable thing.

CHAP LAU CHU

I.

One day we'll take them down again.
In this city you'd be lucky
if the roof you put up outlasts
the kids you raise. Show me a square
of earth and I will show you where
we put to bed what could have been
walls, a room – an everything. In
a year or two they'll be taller
than before, pushing right up through
the sky. Yes, the kids, too. I swear.

II.

You say compare here and Dawson?
Dawson is a muddy area.
You know why Tanglin Halt is up
and down, up and down? Not level?
Put it this way, Tanglin Halt here
is solid as rock. Lim Yew Hock's
time, they don't have excavator,
cannot level the ground. But still
must build. That time you not born yet,
they build, so many blocks they build.

III.

The day we move in father puts
his ear to the floor, raps once, twice
with his knuckles till every inch

has been tested, his fingers bruised.
Forgetting myself, I run through
the hall and in a flash he stands –
catches me – lifts me off my feet.
Not so fast, he says, *it's all air.*
Somewhere, someone begins cooking.
Char, steam. A din of kitchenware.

IV.

Okay you know this car park? Next
to the wet market, the road there?
Got one whole row of shophouses,
police, next door got PAP,
now a lot closed already, there?
Behind last time is where we used
to have the getai. You don't see
the car park very small – last time
whole block of people can squeeze there!
All the children one row. That's where.

V.

For a few minutes every night
it's like someone comes by and sets
a flock of pigeons free, all at
once, an act of mercy so brief
and extravagant we want it
to happen again and again.
They're dark at first, flocking between
the blocks, and then suddenly lit
as each door (and ours) swings open –
it's Ma, home from the factory.

VI.

Not say is very crowded lah.
So this is the room right, mattress
on the floor, then three of us sleep
nearer the wall so won't fall down.
That time also got the tenant
from Malaysia, take one room. So
the rest of us, one room. My Mum
and Dad, three of us. Usually
I'll go to the hawker centre –
do homework, sometimes sleep also.

VII.

Morning settles above the field
like a cloud. In places mud has
swallowed the grass, leaving only
little blades sticking up towards
the sky. In some ways it looks just
like a map of the earth – brown, blue
and green, in scattered areas.
Imagine if this is all there was:
easy, from up here. Now look again –
what if this were all there was?

VIII.

Most, move already. Some of them
like my neighbour, that old lady
I told you? Move to Ang Mo Kio.
Ang Mo Kio, you know? Must be it's

cheaper. That time one room one hall,
now change two room one hall. I heard
they will pay you some more, must be
some allowance, help you to move.
The rest of us? Soon lor, don't know
when yet. I don't want to be last.

IX.

For a while there were volunteers,
on the weekends especially,
asking if we needed a hand
with all the packing, some even
staying long enough at the door
to hear all about the estate –
old times, what it was like back then.
Quieter now, the days bring
fewer visitors. And even then,
even this will come to an end.

X.

Nowadays people grow herb, grow
flower, is different. Last time
Japanese come, all we have is
eng chai to eat! You won't know one.
Move here, got fruits. Grow papaya
down at the train tracks, lemongrass
outside my front door. After this
not sure whether still can or not.
Can plant? Where to plant? Actually
don't know. But I say I don't want.

FORTY DAYS

In the end, they say, it takes forty days
to move the shrine, forty days of joining hands
for the tricky climb down by the flyover

picking their way with the light of a phone
step by step to where the tracks dip to silence,
the morning glory still wet on the fence,

as Queensway and Portsdown hoist an arch
of eight lanes overhead throwing their velvet
veil across the gravelly path. Forty days

in this soft crook of the soil, watching
hunched grasses paint large strokes with the sun,
while in a tall papaya's shade nearby two men

tend a garden sprung from seeds once spat
through the shutters of train cabins while they ran.
Forty days, as others at the church might say,

their good Lord spent in the wilderness,
forty days till they heard, from a crack in the wall,
a voice like a small spring singing.

Here it comes, closer, past the old hospital
and mosque, full of thunder and rain – still *now*,
listen – hear it sway the earth again.

THE VIEW

Somewhere a flag is torn from its plastic.
A child ties the strings to a window-grille
and a blood shadow falls across the room.

There is red over everything. The chairs,
which were always beige, and also the floor
which is marble, and washes easily.

Even on television, the men seem
to redden as they troop into sight. Nothing
escapes. Close your eyes, and the darkness

surges with a pinkish hue, which gathers from
both sides like a flood. Hard to see now,
with all this red (that is, if you were one

to celebrate the view before), harder
to imagine how the room could have been
with its softer colours meant to set off

the coastal light. I think of it sometimes –
the low carved table, worn coffee-mugs, and
beyond our open doorway, the corridor.

PART THREE

THE ANGELS

'For You have made him a little lower than the angels...'
– Psalm 8:5

Common enough over the blocks,
we've all seen them or so we think.
More often if we're honest the eye

skates from floor to floor and then
clean beyond, to the next tower
identically towering.

To see them, or more properly
to see the brushstrokes of their wings
embossed upon the air, the mind

must slow, against its will, a net
ballooning into cold water.
If we are quick, they, quickest, will

disappear. No wonder the saints
reaching later for words, described
them shimmering – for that is how

we must seem to ourselves. Always
afoot, never the chance to dive
into the current of our own lives.

THE CHARIOT

My grandmother's hands are spotted like the sun.
Across the needlework an aurora blooms,
stippling the thin surface. Her skin – it ripples
in minute creases, as gauze does
when a single thread has come loose.
I smooth a finger over her pinpricked wrist.

*

In a corner of the room, under the window-ledge:
an emptiness into which her wheelchair
is sometimes folded. A parking-lot. I ask about
what she's kept there throughout my childhood,
so snug in the room's architecture
it occurs to no-one that it's gone. 你的针车呢?
The vowels float up, against the roof of my mouth.
Grandmother stares. I repeat the phrase – *zhen che* –
her needle's chariot, sturdy neck rising curved
and cool to the touch from a wooden deck harnessed
to its Singer frame. *Oh, Kenny must have cleared it*
says Big Aunt, still watching the TV
where the commercials are stitched so seamlessly
you'd think they were part of the show.

*

Already then, we'd found some other use for it,
as a table or as time went by, another flat surface
on which the things of this earth could accumulate.
Its great wheel, which had run great distances
no longer ran, nor would grandmother's foot

ply the brass pedal to ease it from its rust.
On its outstretched wing we piled bedsheets, pillows,
even the cot that dangled one grandson then another
from the ceiling, a fold in the fabric all it took
to wrap us up in sleep. These years it slept,
bobbin empty, as we watched over it, or it us,
its one elbow crooked and steadfast over the wood.

*

Gloves. Ma insists they were gloves, though
in the clammy heat I can't fathom why a factory
would've made them here. Easier to picture
the foreman going door to door to hand them out,
all the mothers in the neighbourhood bent
over those round and repeating shapes. Night
after night, feet in the stirrups – and their daughters
dim-lit by a muted serial, waiting to smooth out
the fingers. On either side the pairs pile up
in a bag, *left left right right,* that by the morning
will go to be counted as profit, loss. The image
flickers, though in grandmother's eye I catch
something like a doused spark, know she sees
it too. Wheels turn, somewhere a needle moves.
In her hands a thread goes taut, and runs and runs.

MOVING IN

Through the door before I know it. A sort
of frequency guides the feet across
the tiles, the shedding of shoes, parquet stairs
tensing in small arcs beneath the newspaper,
a memory of workmen ascending
and descending with charts in hand, slow
assembly of shelves, parts to call a life.
Our life. Here in the house which has been
made new, a day's weight slung unevenly
across the shoulders, I move surely past
dining chairs, an easel, past the landing
and the elbow of a banister, feel
the cool spreading from where wood makes way
for vinyl, my hand missing the switch
in the wall before suddenly an edge
of must fills the nostrils, and in that fog
are the shapes of boxes haphazardly
arrayed, barest outline of a room
that was once my own but is now spare.
What visits, unsparing, on the present
is not the past but some appendix of it,
this self-that-was that still haunts the ramparts,
lingers to take in a familiar view.
My fingers find the lights – *away with ghosts* –
and in the bright contours of your furniture
and mine, sprightly in plastic, the yet-unwrapped
pictures waiting their turn, all other lives
recede, all other houses which are this house,
a map of streets laid and laid over, belonging
not to the day's but the night's commonwealth.

DE PARADISO

according to PropertyGuru

has 20 floors, freehold, in District 12, Balestier,
and is a relatively new condominium in the area.

Developed by Citiraya in 2005,
it has all the amenities required for the modern-day life –

all the essentials like 24 hours security, a pool,
5 shopping places, 3 MRTs, 4 good quality schools.

It has an amazing barbecue area for the food lovers
and an amazing jacuzzi for the comfort loving.

Another thing which is amazing is its connectivity
keeping in mind the requirements of the upcoming century,

Novena Square has supermarkets, retail outlets, restaurants,
entertainment facilities, banks, eating establishments,

and Novena MRT is only 0.9km away
(business hub in 10 mins on vehicles via Expressway).

What makes it best among the available options
is its unique design and development.

On average, there are 3 units on every floor,
which makes the building quite luxurious, single tower,

all are perfectly comfortable and have a terrace
which gives perfect sunshine and breeze.

3 bedrooms, 2 bathrooms (1130 sq ft).
Everything can be taken care of within a minute.

REPORT FROM A CITY UNDER LOCKDOWN

after Dante's Inferno

Westwards one afternoon. In the hot hours
roads roam with ghosts, making the trees quiver,
blocks like paper hoarding fizzle into view.
No-one at the crosswalks, though the lights
cycling through their changes believe otherwise.
Is this how it is? To pass the finish

and see houses, cars, sent ahead of us
slip earth's surly bonds and reappear
through the fire to fill this, our underworld?
Bright sun curves the emptiness like a sheet,
tucks our vision in around the edges
as highway hunkers to join exit

at Clementi, Toh Tuck, Jalan Bahar,
a strange blue streaking off-screen on the satnav.
High-rises make way for container parks
whose messengers on their great haunches roll
clean through the soul's depot. The road to hell,
it's said, could've been better paved

especially in the wet season, when
potholes brim at a threat of rain. This then
is how a city ends, not with a bang
but six lanes braiding in a roundabout,
eternal repose of toll road and flyover.
Beyond this, numbered streets reach tenderly

in elliptical loops toward the sea
which laps restless around an island's brink
as factories sit swaddled in the dust.
Silent, and not just for a season,
their signs still boast of things made to last:
our hard-nosed striving and our industry.

PSALM FOR A PANDEMIC

Left to themselves, the shapes of all green things
begin to describe their own flourishing.

A field rouses itself into a mist,
a shimmer of birds among its tallest

grasses. From bridges, the bougainvillea
let their long hair down. Kerbside, the verges

surge without remorse. Even the trees
are no longer wood but water – like the sea

unshored they spill out over the pavement,
catch our feet in their slow accoutrements.

Iron gives way to ivy. Where are the
hard words now, of our roadsigns and hazards?

As hair gone uncut, the whole earth thickens.
We can be kind too, if they let us.

THE TWO BRAVEST HUMANS

'Singapore began its vaccination exercise [last December],
with healthcare workers the first to get the shots…'
– Channel NewsAsia

Mother goes first, says it's nothing, is back
on her rounds the morning after. So much

for fear. Her patients don't know what it is
she's done but that it brings her back, nurses

too, Mondays Thursdays and Fridays with those
boxes of pills. Sometimes no-one else comes

so they're all there is, wrapped up in their gloves
and gowns, dispensing cheer. Next is Father's

and–since it hasn't been that long, really
since his sickness went away – we only

pretend not to worry. But that same week
he's back at it, full swing, his clinic packed

straight through the balmy mornings. At dinner
one night someone says *maybe wait and see,*

something about side effects taking months
to show. Others nod their heads, *just so much*

we don't know. It's still light when I get up
to leave, but all I can see is the two

of them at home, one standing, the other
at the kitchen table painting, brown soft

strokes of a face, two faces, the two
bravest humans though they'd never say so.

'MAY 1954' AT THE INTERNATIONAL SCHOOL

Minutes to the bell and they're not having it,
feet wagging, fingers drumming the dull beat

of a Friday afternoon. Bespectacled Khir
stifles a giggle as he reads – *depart*

Tom, Dick, and Harry – not out of shyness,
but because he can already hear the boys

in the lift, what fun they'll have with the words.
I press on: tell them about how the poet

though not much older than they, was pulled
at the crack of dawn from his bed, stood

trial for a magazine; say something
about the power of language to summon

events from the march of time, set things
in motion... the air-conditioning

creaks, somewhere a table drags across the tiles
and suddenly the spell is broken. History

spills around me into the corridor,
dammed-up joy unstopped by the end of the hour

as I fold my lesson-notes into my bag –
sometimes it doesn't repeat itself, but nags.

NILA

[…] in the fifty-fifth year he came alone,
having fled the court of his upbringing
& flung his crown into the solvent waves
& was found in the company of strong men
(who, like him, spoke a language of their joy)
& began to build the city that he'd seen
in the dreams of his father and his brothers
or heard of, in the tales of those returning:
which lifted its towers high against heaven
& draped its flag like a bloodstain on the sky
& became proud, for having hauled itself
from the sea, to stand on borrowed sand
yet offered no room to lay his kingly head
nor servant's wage, to redeem his father's name
& bound him wholly to the promise of his fate –
still he built, with the inheritance of his hands
the foundations of this distant city's fame
& took heart, with each sounding of the gong
& with his brothers slept, and hardly ate, till
from the dreaming another kingdom called,
where his son, he knew, had come of age
& finding no house to call his own, would
follow none else but the fortunes of his father
& seek a living in the city boldly named
by a prince that a storm once washed ashore.

MERAH

'Sea charts distinguish between the red cliffs of Tanah Merah
and Bedok... a prominent landmark for navigators and
pilots up to the 19th century'
– Kwa Chong Guan

...and longer ago: a late sumatra

sidling up the coast, crackling and harmless
for as long as the red earth stood over us.

Along the toothy shore one could stand
in water calm as glass, or sand, as this queen

of storms came calling across the open sea
with freight from as far as the world seemed then,

king's yellow, ivory-black, lapis blue.
And still nothing would match its russet hue...

[1603]

Write, Grotius: how they waited all night
in our shallows, drinking salt

as our swamps drove the Catarina to her loss,
how not one of us in our houses

turned to look, opened the windows even,
knowing our own mare liberum [1]

had changed hands for so much smoke,
so much metal. Early the next

morning we saw her towed against the wind
trailing our finest incense behind

her, a cloud. Write: how much hung in the
balance. Our water. *Our air.*

   [1819]

(A premonition, then,

   [1942]

      of what on earth would come, again.)

   [1956]

He called the house *Tumasek,* but of course
we came to know it by its address, *Besar,* [2]
for it was larger than life, as he himself was;

large, also, of heart. Only years later did
we hear (too late) the echo of those cliffs
cut down to size, a rumble in his voice

that never went away, whose very ground
had been pulled from under him. It was this
he considered the greatest theft: wide water –

once visible from where he'd sit, holding
court – now beyond reach, and in its place
another port, its laden ships, their rise and fall.

   [1994]

East Meadows. The Glades. Country Park.
Eastwood Regency. D'Manor. Limau Park.

Costa del Sol. Parbury Hill. The Baycourt.
Casa Merah. Palmwoods. Stratford Court.

The Springfield. The Clearwater. Tropicana.
Urban Vista. Tanamera Crest. Tanamera.

[...]

Now everything comes from this   the new blocks
draped fluttering red   over their faux brick shade
the levelled lie of the land   even the new terminal
where the sea pours in   from over tall steel sides

also the school that has been built   called temasek
the field that has taken over   the swimming pool
so that not a trace exists   of even that bleached sea
of learning to swim   and through the sting, to see

in time perhaps even I   will say I come from this
singing this orphaned soil   the only tongue I know
from where the rain still gathers   when it arrives
from where the earth rises still higher   in my sleep.

---

1.   'The Sea is common to all, for it is so limitless that it cannot become the possession of any one.' – Hugo Grotius, *Mare Liberum*; after the Dutch East India Company's capture of Portuguese carrack *Santa Catarina* off the coast of Tanah Merah.

2.   David Marshall, first Chief Minister of Singapore and founder of the Workers' Party, lived at 48A, Tanah Merah Besar Road.

FROM A FIELD

I.

something rises,
harrying the grass –
a cloud the height of trees.

Before our eyes
the earth gives up its water,
wavers. Where stood
the cobbler's shelf
now this apparition, this
watermark

level with the air,
levels with the air.

II.

Once barely wide enough
the road, shorn of its buildings
has grown to fill the space
under the awnings:
it is the view.

A sign puts its foot down.
Block 46-2, 46-3
and then a little arrow
as if all it took were to look
harder in that direction.

But squinting does no good.

Beyond the shaved road –
so many coarse blades
fielding the sun's rays.

III.

Further afield
is where we've all come from,
sitting with our backs turned
against the glare. Cars
cooling in the morning's heat,
tea cooling on a platter,
clack of enamel or earthenware

on a tile countertop. Fibreglass,
melamine, green
on green on green.

IV.

It's hard to look away, after all
from something unfinished

the way a leaf vacating
an old rain tree
still stops the gaze, though the ending
is forgone.

Where others have fallen
onto the narrow road
someone has swept them into neat drifts,
leaving a path

or a space, as one created by a force,
a field.

V.

After the rain
at a snail's pace
they bear their belongings away.

For the crows,
a field day.

WHERE THEY BURN BOOKS

'So that grass doesn't grow over history' – *Wolfram P. Kastner*

Set fire to earth again:
it is a new year,
and grass has sprung
in silence over the place
of wrong.

The year is 1933
and good intentions
are licking the concrete.
Look, they dance
on the square with feet

like the young. Words go
as fuel
in the crack of a match –
how quickly the flame comes,
how easily it takes!

With greater difficulty
you and I
torch a fresh circle onto the lawn.
What a hardy thing grass is,
and handy to build on.

*'Singapore has had many visitors in the way of circuses, but
rarely has a more clever show visited the town than now
performing on the Raffles Reclamation Ground...'*
– The Straits Times

No, play it again –
     a circus handler leaves a gate unlatched
a hired watchman looks the other way
     a serving-boy stoops silent on a stair
as a teacher aims, maims the teak table.
     No-one awake to sight the telltale pelt:
only a barman skimming a potted tale
     embellished with the spices of the fleet
to men ashore. Here the scent of a shot
     lingers, like skin on a wall – it is how
it is in the tropics – it is the plot.

*

TIGER SHOOTING EXTRAORDINARY
Singapore Free Press and Mercantile Advertiser

Last Sunday some Kling showmen brought a
FULLY GROWN TIGER over here from Johore
which they exhibited in a show tent
on the Beach Road reclamation site. Late
the same night the WILD ANIMAL broke loose
and for two days has been ROAMING AT LARGE
having defied all efforts at capture.

*

In one version, I am asleep:
in true Oriental fashion (newspaper says) *he*
did not trouble himself to find out what it was.
     The truth – if you'd been there,
seen a tongue's red gash steeping the felt carpet
heard a chain rattling like a tail across the floor
     you'd know. There was no need
and in any case it fixed me on the stair, that glare
a song of songs, last will and testament, or a dare –

*

In 1902, the last tiger that was killed in Singapore
was pursued at Raffles Hotel Singapore.

A colleague saw the tiger and requested the help
of a headmaster who was known

to be a hunter and a sharp shooter. It was dark
and with his loaded gun, he fired

three missed shots at the tiger. The right opportunity
for him to redeem his reputation

came when he caught the gleaming eyes of the tiger.
As bystanders approached the body,

the tiger's head rose. He pulled his trigger again
and the last tiger in Singapore finally

laid its head to rest under the Bar & Billiard Room.
rafflessingapore.com/the-raffles-stories.

*

Build us a room, they said, and let it be
known in the distant corners of these parts
for its fine proportions, state-of-the-art
(and in time, we hope, for its clientele).

'Observe its equal columns, cool interior
providing respite from the noontime sun,
felt on the tables, fresh-chalked cues… even
the floor, raised to level the playing-field.

A room for gentlemen of some distinction,
but not out of reach to a second son.'
Could it be done? Yes, and so we made
one open on all sides to a sailor's breeze,

sanded the floor till it shone like the moon
on an August night. Which is to say, one
we'd never dream of entering. A room
to shoot the breeze. A room to put them right.

*

These days one can buy a figurine at
the hotel store, find a likeness printed
on cards and aprons. In children's books
it gazes friendly from the page, beside
the grazing humans. No-one tells the story –
how once upon a colonial morning
a beast, hunted, haunted instead. Now
the red brickwork's painted black, silent hands
scrub these chalky walls. Still, some days that's all
it takes. A half-glimpsed coat or mane, a flame
to put a fire under this room again.

ALLEGORY OF RAIN

After silence, heat. And after heat it falls,
falls; will not be held against its will, drains
the sky blue. Gone from the air, its weight
takes new shape from rifts in the soil,

blunts blades of grass, by swelling in places
moves the brown earth to make a way. How
gladly it runs underfoot. On another
island which has come to silence they say,

be like water. Here, where we once thought
the rains were scarce, we sit at round tables
and await each coming party, their clean
smiles, cameras eager as promises. What

we know, we know. Not from this sound or
fury, but a wisdom in our hands: how water
put to boil makes the charred grounds sing.
How suddenly storms come to dance on zinc.

'Clearances' and 'Relocations' make use of direct quotes from Notices of Possession served under the Land Acquisition Act by the Housing and Development Board (HDB). 'Clearances' also quotes from an advertisement placed on 12 March 1857 in the *Singapore Free Press and Mercantile Advertiser,* which was founded by William Napier.

Portions of 'Relocations' borrow from oral history and archival records presented by Loh Kah Seng in his thesis, 'The 1961 Kampong Bukit Ho Swee Fire and the Making of Modern Singapore' (Murdoch University, 2008); as well as my own family's memories of the 1968 fire at Bukit Ho Swee.

Separately, sections of 'Relocations', as well as 'Chap Lau Chu', are based on the oral histories of former residents of Tanglin Halt, collected by the non-profit organization My Community and made available for my research. The sequence was first presented as a hybrid performance titled 'Dis/Locations', in collaboration with singer-songwriter Vivien Yap at the Esplanade.

'The Gardener' was commissioned by Raffles Institution for commissioned by Raffles Institution for the school's bicentennial, and also published in *Some Dreams From Now* (Pagesetters, 2023).

'Studio Photograph Of A Chinese Man In Fancy Costume' and 'Commonwealth' are responses to photographs in the National Archives of Singapore collection (Negative nos. 93,524/27 and A4924/14 respectively). The former includes excerpts from *Stay True*, a memoir by Hua Hsu (Doubleday, 2022) and the film *Talking Leaves* by Shubigi Rao (presented at the ArtScience Museum in 2022), both reproduced with permission.

The epigraph to 'Quarantine' is taken from Lee Kuan Yew's memoir, *The Singapore Story* (Simon & Schuster, 1998). 'De Paradiso' is a found poem, based on the condominium's listing on PropertyGuru. Both these poems, along with 'Report From A City Under Lockdown', were commissioned for *Divining Dante* (Recent Work Press, 2021) to mark the 700th anniversary of Dante's death. The anthology was jointly edited by Paul Munden and Nessa O'Mahony, along with guest editors Alvin Pang, Paul Hetherington, David Fenza, Priya Sarukkai Chabria, and Moira Egan.

'Funan: A Travellers' Guide' is one of the source texts for composer Jonathan Shin's 'Three City Ballads', which premiered in July 2024.

'Sentence' was commissioned for *No News*, edited by Paul Munden and Alvin Pang (Recent Work Press, 2020).

'Yellowtop' was written in memory of my grandfather, Tay Chong Yam.

'This Year' was commissioned by StAnza Festival as part of the WindowSwap project in 2021.

'Seniors' Activity Corner' was commissioned by Candlestick Press in 2019, and later republished in *A Given Grace*, edited by Desmond Kon and Eric Valles (Squircle Line Press, 2021).

'Corridor' was commissioned by The Arts House for the Note for Note programme in 2021.

'Forty Days' references the removal and relocation of the Sri Thandavaalam Muneeswaran Alayam shrine, originally sited along the KTM railway tracks near Tanglin Halt, as requested by the Singapore Land Authority in 2017. The shrine's treasurer at the time, Mr Adaikalam Annadhurai, said it would take 40 days of prayers to appease the railway god ahead of the relocation.

'The Chariot', written for my grandmother, Tan Ai Iu, was placed second in the Welsh International Poetry Competition 2024. 'The Swimmers' is also written for her.

'"May 1954" at the International School' was written after a class taught at Invictus International School, and references a poem by Edwin Thumboo.

'Where They Burn Books' responds to the artist Wolfram Kastner's annual act of burning a circle into the Königsplatz lawn, to mark the Nazi book burnings of 10 May 1933. I shared the poem with Kastner, who replied – "it is always and everywhere necessary to [protect] the culture of humanism, peace, and freedom".

ACKNOWLEDGEMENTS

This book dwells on a series of dislocations and relocations in the Commonwealth district of Singapore, broadening its gaze to how colonialism has shaped the island's built and human geographies, over two centuries since Stamford Raffles's landing.

These parallel and intertwined histories – of Commonwealth and the British commonwealth – have marked the lives of generations of residents.

I am grateful to the historian Dr Loh Kah Seng for his research on the fires at Kampong Bukit Ho Swee during the 1960s, as well as to members of my own maternal family for sharing their recollections. The years I spent in my grandmother's home, growing up, are inseparable from every memory I have of Tiong Bahru, Alexandra and Queenstown. This book is for her, too.

I am also indebted to the nonprofit organisation My Community for granting me access to the oral histories of former residents of Tanglin Halt and Commonwealth Drive, who have similarly experienced relocation in recent years.

Other poems draw on material from the National Library and National Archives of Singapore, part of a rich digitized collection that is freely accessible online.

As ever, thanks to Carcanet Press for the care and attention that have gone into the making of this book, and for championing poetry and poets in the UK and far beyond.

Finally, deepest thanks to the editors of the following publications, where some of these poems first appear:

A Given Grace (Squircle Line Press, 2021), *Alluvium, Anthropocene Poetry, Bath Magg, Bombay Review, Contour: A Lyric Cartography of Singapore* (Ethos Books, 2019), *Dark Mountain, Gutter Magazine, InkLinks, The London Magazine, Mekong Review, Modern Poetry in Translation, No News* (Recent Work Press, 2020), *Pace Journal, Poetry International, Journal of Practice, Research & Tangential Activities (PR&TA), Quarterly Literary Review of Singapore, Rabbit Poetry, Some Dreams From Now* (Pagesetters, 2023), *Tiger Moth Review,* and *Write Where We Are Now* (Manchester Metropolitan University, 2020).